At the Fitness Center

by Cecilia Winters
illustrated by Jane McCreary

Practice Decodable 53

Mc Graw Hill Education

Bothell, WA • Chicago, IL • Columbus, OH • New York, NY

MHEonline.com

McGraw-Hill Education

Send all inquiries to:
McGraw-Hill Education
8787 Orion Place
Columbus, OH 43240

ISBN: 978-0-02-135461-0
MHID: 0-02-135461-8

Printed in China.

8 9 10 11 12 DSS 27 26 25 24 23

Grace visited the fitness center.
First, Grace exercised.

Then Grace raced in circles.
That was fun!

Next Grace swam and swam.
Grace swam fast.

Then Grace did flips on bars.
And she did tricks on them.

Grace ended her visit at dance class.
Then she made a call on her cell.

"I am tired!" Grace said.

"I will not make you walk" said Mom.